CONTENTS

THE STORY OF PIRATES

Pirates are sea robbers. Throughout history they have terrorised the world's seas. Wherever there have been ships with goods worth stealing, there have been pirates.

THE GOLDEN AGE OF PIRACY

The 1600's and early 1700's were known as the Golden Age of Piracy. Two earlier events had greatly changed the history of piracy. One was the discovery of a sea route from Europe to India. The other was the discovery of America.

These finds opened up an exciting new world for European trade. Ships were sent to India, Arabia and America. There they were loaded with goods such as gold, tobacco, silks and spices, and then sailed back to Europe. Not surprisingly, the temptation to rob these ships of their new found wealth was one that many could not resist.

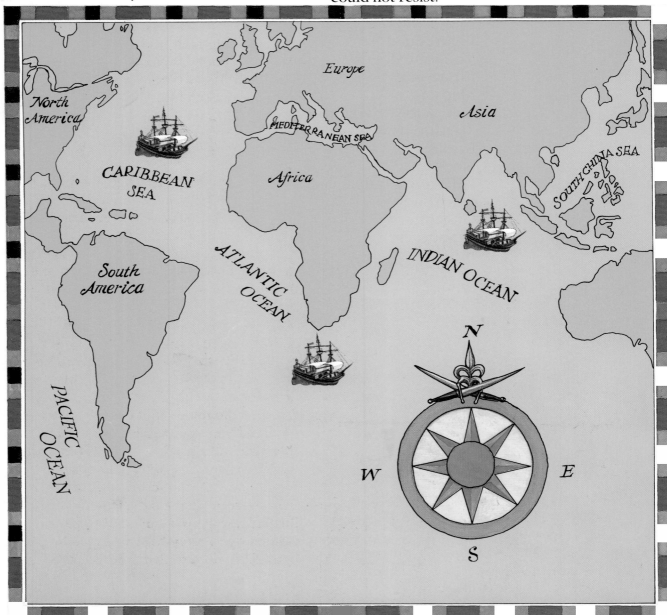

CRAFT TOPICS

PIRATES

FACTS ● THINGS TO MAKE ● ACTIVITIES

RACHEL WRIGHT

W
FRANKLIN WATTS
LONDON ● SYDNEY

© 1991 Franklin Watts
This edition 2002

Franklin Watts
96 Leonard Street
London
EC2A 4XD

Franklin Watts Australia
56 O'Riordan Street
Alexandria, Sydney
NSW 2015

ISBN 0 7496 4553 9 (pbk)

Dewey Decimal Classification 364.1

Editor: Hazel Poole
Designer: Sally Boothroyd
Photographer: Chris Fairclough

A CIP catalogue record for this book is
available from the British Library

Printed in Dubai

MAPMAKING

You will need: paper ● waterproof pens or coloured pencils ● a used tea bag ● cooking oil and brush ● kitchen paper.

2. To make your map look ancient, tear the edges slightly. Gently wipe both sides of your map with a used damp tea bag. Crumple it into a ball and leave it to dry.

1. Draw a map of an island and choose where you would bury your treasure. Don't forget landmarks such as trees, mountains and rivers. They will help to guide you.

3. When your map is dry, uncurl it, put it on a sheet of paper, and brush it carefully with cooking oil. Then blot it dry with kitchen paper. It should now look and feel more like genuine parchment.

Did you know that Blackbeard is said to have buried treasure on a remote island and then left one of his fourteen wives there, alone, to guard it?

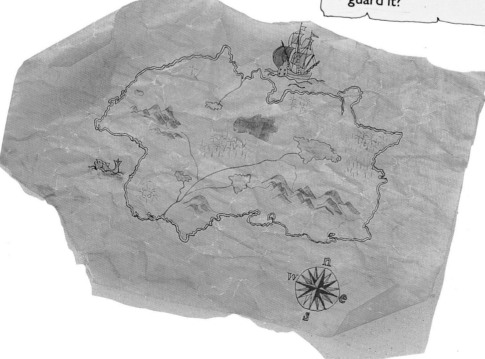

Bake a Pirate Island

You will need: poster paints and brushes ● plastic drinking straws ● old pasta shells or dried beans ● toothpicks ● coloured card ● tissue paper ● glue.
Island dough recipe: 250g old plain white flour; 100g salt; 2 tablespoons of cooking oil; water; mixing bowl. You will also need to ask an adult to help you.

1. Mix the flour and salt in a large mixing bowl. Add the oil and just enough water to make a soft dough. Knead well and then divide the dough into two lumps.

2. Shape one lump into an island. You might like to add mountains, rock pools and caves. Or even a hidden bay where your ship could lurk, ready for a surprise attack. Use the remaining dough to make a skeleton, a ship or anything else you might find on or near a pirate island.

3. Line a baking tray with foil and bake your models in the oven for about 25 minutes at Gas Mark 4 (350°F/180°C). If you want them rock hard, leave them in a little longer.

4. When your models have cooled, start painting! Decorate your beaches with dried beans or painted pasta shells. Draw bones on to your skeleton!

5. If you made a ship base, cut out sail shaped pieces of card and glue them on to toothpicks. Now, stick them into your ship. Don't forget to add a pirate flag!

6. To make palm trees, twist folded squares of tissue paper into shortened straws. Open out the paper slightly and tear the edges to make it look more like leaves. If your island is very hard, gently drill a hole in it with a toothpick. Then plant your palm tree in the hole.

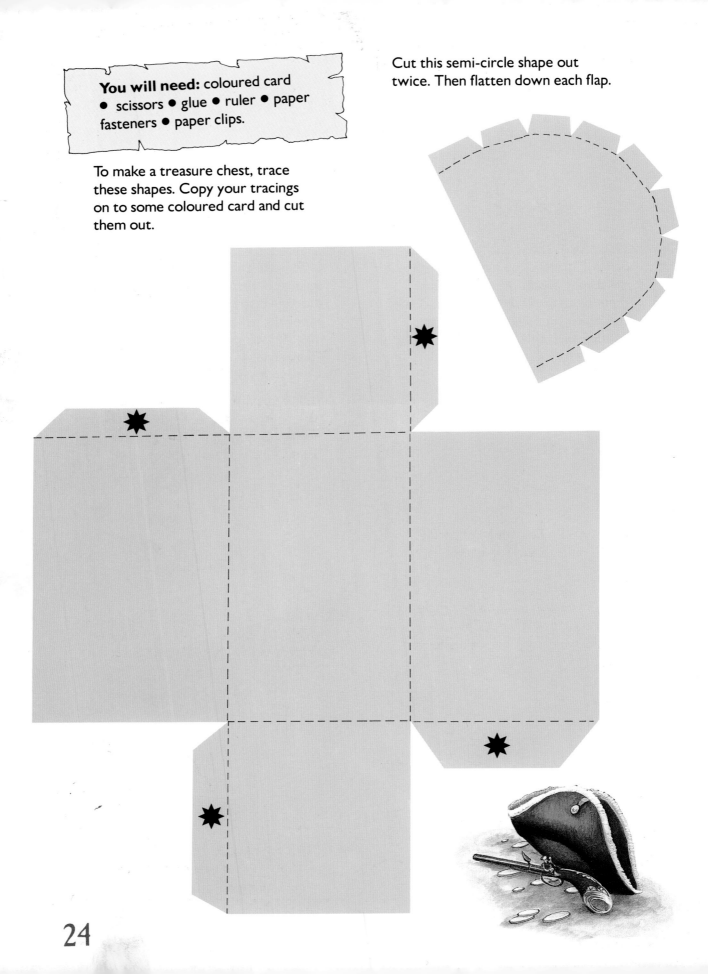

You will need: coloured card ● scissors ● glue ● ruler ● paper fasteners ● paper clips.

To make a treasure chest, trace these shapes. Copy your tracings on to some coloured card and cut them out.

Cut this semi-circle shape out twice. Then flatten down each flap.

24

TREASURE CHEST

1. To make a box, glue the back of each flap marked * on to its nearest panel.

2. To make the lid, cut a rectangle of card 14cms by 8cms. Put a strip of glue along one of the longer sides.

3. Holding your rectangle like this, stick it to the flaps of one of your semi-circles.

4. It helps if you paper clip these two pieces together while waiting for the glue to dry. Now, glue the other semi-circle into place.

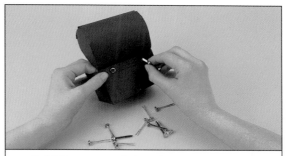

5. When your lid is dry, use paper fasteners to attach it to the chest.

6. Decorate the chest with strips of a different coloured card fixed with paper fasteners.

KNOTS

If you worked on a sailing ship you really did have to "know the ropes". The masts and sails were controlled by a mass of ropes called rigging. Like all sailors, pirates needed to know exactly where each rope was and how it was tied. Here are two knots the pirates in this book might have used.

The Reef Knot — good for joining two ends of rope over a reefed, or rolled up, sail.

The Cat's Paw — ideal for attaching a rope to a hook.

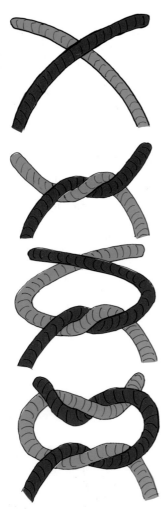

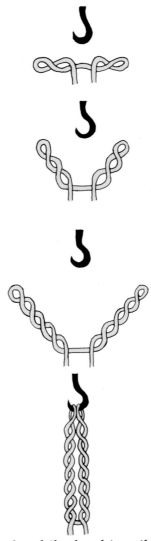

To measure the speed of their sailing ships, pirates of old would probably have used a log line. This was a length of cord, knotted at equal spaces, with a wooden board fixed to one end. The board was thrown into the sea. It held the end of the cord steady while the ship sailed on. As the cord unravelled, the pirate holding it would have to count how many knots passed through his fingers in a given time. Each knot equalled the speed of one nautical mile an hour.

SHANTIES

Shanties were work songs, sung by sailors. The earliest ones we know about are well over 200 years old.

With their strong simple rhythms, shanties helped sailors keep in time with each other as they worked.

Different shanties accompanied different tasks. Some with long repetitive rhythms were sung when turning the capstan to haul up the anchor. Others with a short, jerky beat were better suited to working the pumps to get rid of water below deck.

One More Day

On - ly one more day, my John-ny, One more day! Oh, come
rock and roll me o ver One more day!

1   Only one more day, my Johnny,
    One more day;
    Oh, rock and roll me over,
    Only one more day

2   Don't you hear the Old Man
    howling?

3   Don't you hear the mate a-
    growling?

4   No more gales or heavy weather.

5   Only one more day together.

6   Can't yer hear them gals a-calling?

7   Pack your bag today, my Johnny.

Paddy Doyle's Boots

Tim - me way, ay - ay - ay high - ya! We'll
pay Pad - dy Doyle for his BOOTS!

1   To my way-ay-ay-ah
    We'll pay Paddy Doyle for his boots.

2   To my way-ay-ay-ah
    We'll all throw dirt at the cook.

3   To my way-ay-ay-ah
    We'll all drink brandy and gin.

DIFFERENT PIRATES

TRUE PIRATES

True pirates stole from anyone. They were criminals and if caught, faced certain death. Many British pirates ended up hanging from Execution Dock in Wapping, London. Their dead bodies were then chained up along the River Thames as a warning to anyone else thinking of doing a bit of pirating in their spare time.

BUCCANEERS

During the 1600's, a group of runaway men — slaves, criminals and refugees — were living in the Caribbean. Mainly English, French and Dutch, they were a wild, unruly bunch. They hated the Spanish, who ruled much of the Caribbean at that time and so enjoyed plundering Spanish ships whenever they could.

Their name — buccaneers — came from the french word "boucaner", the name of the smoking process when cooking meat, that left a distinctive aroma on the men.

PRIVATEERS

Sailing in ships sponsored by their government back home, privateers had permission to rob ships from enemy countries. The only drawback was that if they managed to return to their own country, they had to share their stolen cargo with their sponsor.

Privateers carried documents called letters of marque. These letters could save them from punishment if their piratical attacks failed. A bit unfair really since their crimes were like that of any other pirate.

DID YOU KNOW?

One of the few things pirate ships had in abundance was rope. So, apart from all its usual uses, pirates wiped their hands with it, greased it to use as candles and tarred strands of it and squeezed them between the ship's planks to stop leaking.

"Walking the plank" is the most famous piratical punishment that never was! There is no proof that this dastardly practice ever existed. Instead, it was probably dreamt up by Victorian story tellers. Or maybe the myth dates back to ancient Roman times when captives not worth holding to ransom were invited to swim ashore.

Pirate ships didn't have a ship's cat, either. A cat would have eaten the ship's rats which the pirates might have wanted to eat themselves. After all, there's a lot of protein in a rat!

At the bottom of the Pacific Ocean, off the coast of South America, lies the largest pirate treasure of all. Hundreds of bits of silver, on board a Spanish ship, were captured by pirates. Mistaking them for tin, the pirate crew threw them overboard. It was later revealed that this lost booty was worth over £150,000!

At one time, Port Royal in Jamaica was a popular pirate haunt. But on June 7 1692 a terrible disaster took place. An earthquake shook the town, the ground opened and whole streets disappeared. As if that was not enough, a huge tidal wave then rushed in and the whole town vanished. Even today divers still find relics from this lost town.

Did you know that all these are other names for a pirate?

Filibusterer
Freebooter
Corsair
Sea Rover

29

GLOSSARY

Amputate, to — to cut off, usually referring to an arm or leg. Sailors of old who had to have limbs amputated were often given swigs of alcohol to help numb the pain.

Articles — rules that pirates and privateers had to obey whilst on board ship. These rules included how any booty was to be divided, and how the ship's captain should be elected.

Barnacles — tiny hard-shelled creatures that cling to a ship's hull. To get rid of them, pirates had to beach their ships (preferably somewhere well hidden), turn them on to one side and scrape the barnacles off. This was called careening.

Bilge — the bottom of a ship. The bilge was packed with stone which helped to keep the ship steady and upright.

Black Jack — another name for the pirate flag. A jack is a flag, especially one flown from the bowsprit of a ship.

Booty — stolen goods.

Bowsprit — a pole projecting from the bow, front part, of a ship.

Buccaneer — a pirate who preyed on Spanish shipping in the Caribbean during the 1600's and 1700's.

Capstan — a revolving wooden cylinder, used for winding up an anchor. Pushing the capstan round was tiring work.

Cargo — goods carried by a ship.

Cat o' nine tails — a whip with nine knotted ropes attached, used for punishing sailors. Those troublemakers who really misbehaved could be sentenced to one hundred lashes or more.

Galley — a ship which had both oars and sails: a ship's kitchen.

Gunwale (gunnel) — upper edge of a ship's side.

Hold — place where a ship's cargo is stored. Water barrels, salted meat, spare ropes and sails would all have been stored here.

Jolly Roger — a pirate flag. Some think that the name, Jolly Roger, may have come from *Old Roger*, another name for the devil. Others believe that it may have come from the French, *joli rouge,* meaning *pretty red* — a reference to the red flags buccaneers used to fly.

Letter of marque — a license, issued by a government, giving the bearer permission to rob enemy ships. These letters sometimes proved to be fakes. If caught with a fake letter, a privateer could be punished as a pirate.

Loot — stolen goods; plunder.

Maroon, to — to abandon someone on a desolate shore. Many pirates feared this punishment more than any other.

Oakum — strands of tarred rope which were squeezed between a ship's wooden planks to stop leaking. Unpicking ropes to make oakum was a very boring job.

Pike — a pointed pole, good for poking at an enemy as you boarded their ship.

Plunder — stolen goods; booty: to rob.

Privateer — a person, or privately owned vessel, authorised to attack enemy ships. Two English privateers, Sir Francis Drake and Sir John Hawkins, were so successful that they were knighted by Queen Elizabeth I.

Prize — a captured ship: booty.

Ransom — money or goods paid for the release of a hostage.

Rigging — system of ropes supporting a ship's masts and sails.

Yellow Jack — flag pirates flew when they had disease on board ship.

Weevil — a type of beetle.

RESOURCES

Books to read
Pirates by Karen McWiliams.
Franklin Watts 1989.

A Plunder of Pirates by Scoular Anderson.
Puffin Books 1989.

Pirates edited Harry Knill, illustrated Gregory Irons.
Bellerphon Books 1975.

The Sea Rovers: Pirates, Privateers, and Buccaneers by Albert Marrin.
Atheneum (N.Y.) 1984.

Treasure Island by R.L. Stevenson.
Adventure story of a boy aboard a privateer.

Robinson Crusoe by Daniel Defoe.
A tale based on the true story of Alexander Selkirk. He was a Scottish sailor who was rescued from the island of Juan Fernandez in 1708, after having spent four years there alone.

Places to visit
The Pirate Ships
Tobacco Docks
Wapping
London E1 9SF
Tel: 071 702 9681
(Exhibition of the true story of Piracy — housed in two life-size replica ships).

National Maritime Museum
Greenwich
London SE10 9NF
Tel: 081 858 4422
(Not specifically about pirates, but plenty about the ships they would have sailed in).

There are maritime museums throughout Britain. Contact your local tourist board to find which one is nearest to you.

Games to play
Pirates adventure computer game.
Microprose, Unit 1,
Hampton Road Industrial Estate,
Tetbury, Glos GL8 8LD.

Pirate High Seas adventure game.
Rickitt Educational Media,
Ilton, Ilminster,
Somerset, TA19 9HS

Index